Sight is No Carpenter

Sight is No Carpenter

Poems by Art Homer

CustomWords

© 2005 by Art Homer

Published by CustomWords
P.O. Box 541106
Cincinnati, OH 45254-1106

Typeset in Goudy by WordTech Communications LLC, Cincinnati, OH

ISBN: 1932339957
LCCN: 2004117825

Poetry Editor: Kevin Walzer
Business Editor: Lori Jareo

Visit us on the web at www.custom-words.com

Cover art: Leland Sherwood
Photo credit, cover art: Ken Anderson
Photo credit, author photo: Alison Wilson

Acknowledgments

Grateful acknowledgment is made to the following publications in which these poems originally appeared, some in slightly different form.

"Full Immersion Baptism" in *The Poetry Miscellany*; "County Road 142," *Midwest Quarterly*; "Autumn Walk, The Old Neighborhood," *Writer's Forum*; "A Heart Attack in the Men's Shower," *The Southern Review*: "Winter Sonnet for an Absent Friend," *Prairie Schooner*; " "Wedge-Tailed Eagles," *North American Review*; "Mary Cassatt: The Bath," *Tar River Poetry*; "Kingbird," *New Letters*; "The New Docent's Tour of Bathtub Madonnas, South Omaha," "The Home I've Never Seen," *American Literary Review*; "Blowhole and Green Glass at the Apostles," *Chariton Review*; "Homeplace," "Breaking," "A Why-Not of Stones," "Driving," "Walking to Work," *Colorado Review*; "The Value of Art," *Kansas Quarterly*; "Late Portrait of Robert," *Southern Poetry Review*; "Cottonwood Blue" *Poetry*; "I-80 with Charles Darwin," *Prairie Schooner*; "A Font for Alison," *A Garland for Harry Duncan* (W Thomas Taylor, 1989); "To The *Locus Coeruleus*," "For the New Parents," *JAMA: Journal of the American Medical Association*; "Verdigris Creek with Friends," *Connecticut Review*; "Summer 1992, Sarpy County," *Columbia: a Magazine of Poetry & Prose*;

For Alison

Contents

I-80 with Darwin & Other Journeys
I-80 with Charles Darwin 13
To the *Locus Coeruleus* 15
Verdigris Creek with Friends 17
First Cast 19
Hatchery Trout on the High Plains 20
Summer 1992, Sarpy County 21
Cottonwood Blue 23
County Road 142 25
Breaking 26
Driving 28
Walking to Work 30
Autumn Walk, the Old Neighborhood 31
The Home I've Never Seen 32
Full Immersion Baptism 35
Remembered Shoreline 37
Crossing the Equator at 40 Thousand Feet 39
Dream of Black Water 41
Blowhole and Green Glass at the Apostles 43

A Field Guide to the Birds
Wedge-Tailed Eagles 47
Dunnocks on Norman Graves 48
Guillemots on Cliffs 49
Corncrake in Flooded Fields At Hundred House 50
Oystercatcher on Anglesea 51
Raven in Matthew Price's Field, Hundred House 52
Kingbird 53
Winter Sonnet for an Absent Friend 54

Paintings & Portraits
Homeplace 57
The Rapids 58
A Font for Alison 60
The Value of Art 61
Mary Cassatt: The Bath 62
For the New Parents 64

Late Portrait of Robert 65
The New Docent's Tour of Bathtub Madonnas, South Omaha 67
Paris, a Rainy Day, Rue de This, Rue de That 68
A Why-Not of Stones 70
A Heart Attack in the Men's Shower 71
Execution 73

I-80 with Darwin & Other Journeys

I-80 with Charles Darwin

Illness is just bad weather in my head, a snail's
pace for dry climate where country people think
they breed from dew. Land like this, and times
it's civil if a gentleman sells dirty straw for horses.
Let Darwin do with bones. No bread, but mold
and lichen on the skeletons of mules who carried
ore and died along this road. Why Irish generals
gave names to Spanish towns—*quien sabe?* Something's
wrong with everything or me. My watch is almost up.
Ten till ten, the hands lean northwest. Plain
to mountain, jackrabbit to pipestone, speedometer
rages toward eighty. Highway like a butchershop.
The next town's a line drive for my stomach.

Good eye, Charles, for noticing there's hardly any
hundred yards where nothing grows: lichen, bush, cactus.
We are dormant seeds ourselves, explode in the first
rainy weather. Jealousy is watching mountains
for snowpack, envy of rain at Coquimbo. Here, a dry
mouth, reading the old boys. Sure as small towns,
it's earthquakes to rain, rain to abundance—
some old affection between earth and sky.

One valley is sure some evil brings the mad dogs back.
At the coast, jade swells knock cliffs back underfoot.
Behind us, sheep turn face to turf. It could be
our dogs drive these fat, white swallows off the rocks.
Don't we like running too? Some folks will say . . .

You know what they say: oaks along the river are old
women blown with goiters. Anything. If we take wind
and speed, this inland road for miles, and an eye

for what is right, we'll pick this farm near Pasco
the way a batter picks his ball. As we connect,
the farmwife strains over the pump handle,
proof of children drawn from eighty feet and cold.

To the *Locus Coeruleus*

[One researcher] believes that it is reasonable to look for brain
circuits connected with the emotions.... He has been studying a part
of the brain stem known as the *locus coeruleus,* the 'blue place,' ....
    —from an article on the human brain

I remember you from colder days. We were not
always so comfortable together.
In the wooden room, you would only look
through that window cocked northwest—
toward Mongolia I said—across a cold bay
lit by the same late summer sun that flamed
roofs green and red against a sky
tired as a vein. The floor, pine,
as was the wind-bent ground cover. The sea,
powdery at that latitude.

What needed forgetting in that coast
apartment, I can't remember.
But you, dark corner of my attic,
wouldn't release the strained dusk of eaves.
Bright kites and windsocks shocked
us out of the blue taste of chest ache,
faint blood mist when the coughing passed
(from running too hard in the wind and falling
asleep in the damp dune's grassy lee).

How hard the droplets looked against the sand—
the aerosol of my life like round grains
wind sorted from finer stuff. I touched them,
not sure they were mine, licked them off my fingers.
Was it sea salt I tasted, or cure, iodine and a trace

of smoky driftwood fires? Even the patient
beach horses shied when I leapt from the tussock
to run again. Wind and the slick bullet of hurt

broke from my back. Ocean cold in me, your bite
in my blood, we could have run for days.

Verdigris Creek with Friends

It's spring, but watercress
bites back with the sharp tang of midsummer.
Cabbage the green of Greece, it floats
above tufts of reed and slick surface tension,
a creek bottom sandy enough to wade
without muddying the pools.
My flies bring no rainbow from riprap
of railroad tie and deadfall, so I
practice my roll cast. An awkward
overhand leaves me tied up in sumac.

Downstream, hatchery trout boil through pools,
backs sunburned to the hue of statues,
the copper green that names the creek.
They tie themselves into the letter
for Christ, spell out the oriental
meaning of a preacher's paisley tie.
They are killers and we love them
like the news we hear or make up
of ritual murder two farms
from the bait shop, closed the note says.

"I am out to the hog barn," we read—
"Drive west and honk." When I do,
a dirty blonde girl, six, congeals
from hog funk. A shoat perches
on its pile of spilled feed, and forty
pounds of pit bull chokes on his own snarl,
belly-crawling out to clear
the pickup's differential. The owner,
when he comes, doesn't sell or recommend
flies for this creek, borderline
between tall and short grass prairie.

I am used to coastal streams, evening
rotting comfortably into night,
bats chasing my fly into riffles.
Land this high and light must bind
itself with grass. Pines lean against sky
and bandit cactus bites the foot
I cast into current. I wade singing grass
that flies like the horse of defunct
service stations into a sky painted
red with commerce and strange new stars.

First Cast

Trout and pennyroyal mint strike
the eye with that electric
glint of a battery on the tongue—
metallic, like biting foil or the first
squint of morning through the sparkle
of acacia leaves into sun and lake.
It's no mistake I find myself here
among these silver things, knowing we
wilt quickly in the heat and rely on special
circumstance and sparse rain, take water
near its source and offend as often as please.

At the stream edge, willows shade a bed
of watercress. I cut green twigs to boil
later with the mint. My sore throat and headache
hint at thin skin. A rainbow's belly
flashes and disappears. This whitest flesh
stays firm until cooked, melts into oily
mucilage too strong to eat. This morning
is cool and dry. Sun levers under trees
to boil the dew away. The bruised mint
cools my palms and quickens my first cast.

Hatchery Trout on the High Plains

If wind would stop
hill's breath, grass could tell
these fish their effort
only pumps them through bland stages.
Even here there is room
for the wily one back of the spill.
The big rainbow checks, gills red
slices in the swerve toward food,
as if in afterthought the swarm
of like bodies were enough.

I stand here, a father, over hills
fathomless as water, wondering what
answer a daughter needs to still her
hunger in a distant city of fish and flowers.
If I sing down the river road,
if I travel to the sea in my heart
like a mother, on what anvil will wind
beat me thin enough to glaze
the miles I fish for its ventriloquist
words: Fish Creek, Verdigris. But she
will not hear me and I am still here.

Even the hand must race the arm
to the end of its swing. Like a man
casting coin after coin in a fountain,
I throw my line across unlikely water,
hang my delicate flies in brush.
Trees grab a loose hold on sand
and cactus floors sparse forest.
Dark flycatchers dart from pines,
sure over silver riffles, knowing
their prey and catching it
time after time.

Summer 1992, Sarpy County

No one comes home in this heat. The roads
fill with honest dust we shake from our
feet like pilgrims. Only guests, tenants
of shade and breeze work hard at belief.
Boats lever form and oar in light's face,
the broken line where what cloud there is
slips into solid blade and handle.
Water, sky's torn skin, leaks images
and steals heat. This is the flaw we love
in strangers, forgive so often we
lose parents, children, whole families
town doctors pronounced O.K. Father's
heart was not sound as they'd said, fainting
spells fatal. Paint and the remaining few
bathers peel at the main attraction:
phony beach and lighthouse built before
the war. Miles of land bound corn ignore
the lack of wave, the forlorn beacon
warning only tractors of the blue
land ahead. When relations gather...
(to eat and honor the dead? ... "it would please
your mother...") under the locust tree,
wish for flood. No locust swarms will glove
this land, drive farmers out. It's been ages
since such luck, the local stock grown dull
on milo and church. Three heifers tease
their bulk through a stock pond's dark surface.
Hogs never chew the cud of their grief,

but swallow earth whole, on the one chance
they'll be spared to breed another dour
profit for the dead man's son to hoard.

Cottonwood Blue

If I could forget the plains behind this stand,
forget the train car and how I first saw
brown clouds tabled against a ceiling of heat,
I could imagine this river valley
gave relief to the land, that these tallest trees
diced sky into music above the oxbow
lake where bodies sink surely as pilings
set each spring for temporary docks,
where foundations lower houses like bait
for the leviathan rising of frost.

But it is summer. Useless cottonwoods
do not crack in cold. They've thrown a storm
of pith and down across lawn and screens.
Through field glasses each tree becomes the small
woodland of childhood. This too is dust.
What we imagined when we came here becomes
detritus of wind, the linty pickings of pockets.
Only the eye rejoices at them. Sight is no carpenter,
knows of nothing to do with wood and space
but to call the body out into the evening.

Night is the water we swim, unsafe by nature
of its color and the long light of farms
carrying trains of grain and chemicals east
into the mirror of sunset, dull, unsilvered by heat.
What I have come to remember is not here.
The flat statement of grain elevators rises
across a mile of prairie grass. The mind
circles in flammable dust, considers
an old tautology of feast and vermin, crops
and livestock repeating the expected line.

In last light, the scheduled thunderstorm
comes driving town to dinner, builds
a mountain range to dwarf the land. One butte
collapses into ridge after ridge of night,
a fierce knowledge playing its slopes
long after the dark has fallen
and houselights sink into the earth.

County Road 142
—Appanoose

Sun, having drunk the last of sky's cidery color,
warms a woman standing inexplicably in a soy
field seventeen miles outside Mystic, Iowa.
I finish my roast beef in Brazil and leave a tip.
The fox in a stand of red oak and basswood
has his smells all mixed up by the harvest dust
and wanders into a pack of coyotes by the creek.
Peace and stubble sharpen silence for the farmer
after he's shut the combine off and climbed down
to find those two paws peeking from bean head
blades as if a dog were inside trying to get out.
It doesn't take much more than I know to tell
there's no room for animals as big as gray dogs
in the jammed machinery. Skin, but not much
else is wreathing the cams and gears. I'm losing
my lunch at the turnoff—not because the three
coyotes leapt into the blades. I'm glad the fox
got off. It was just bad beef. The road takes no
good servants but the alert , takes no excuse.
The farmer lays a tongue in the grass, but I upend
the coals of patience and wash out my mouth.

The Amish girl waves roadside thanks a hundred yards
from the pheasant I avoid. Her mother has sewn
bright panels into her dress to make her more visible.
Her white bonnet carries the sweet smoke of her hair
into the wind without spilling any. None of the horses
I see are working the fields though the black buggies
swarm back and forth on fall business. A few pines
on a rise, the last light on the low bluff relieve prairie.
Soon the curl of wind-eddies, snow filled, will reach
into the shallow valleys, rake the cottonwoods—
will claw across ridgepoles of barns, trying hay doors,
the Anabaptist bevels of local faith and joinery.

Breaking

Driving, I break into light,
swallow miles of it.
As after the operation,
pain and violence recalled
deeper than marrow
flap in that net of nerve
memory cannot touch. So
the stunned child spits
his teeth into his hand—
salt an aftertaste in the mouth
of the man who stands for home
by the broken light of his door,
this, the wreck I avoid.
The route home is made
of cloud, dark but for
the gloss of town light.
How the highway slams my back,
the explosions of the pistons
in their infinite runs
down the same track each enough
to tear my arms from sockets
articulated delicately
as the linkages of my car,
all hammering out these miles
for love. I drive
precisely as machines which cast
prosthetic joints for shoulder and hip.

Having held them in my hands,
the alloy sockets perfect,
I can say a man may as well
be metal, crystallized by stress,

may as well be light.
Out of the moon, out of cars

oncoming as the warm light of my foyer,
of light caught between
dark lines of newsprint announcing
Man from Light, Man from Light—
I am breaking.

Driving

Somewhere forgettable in the Midwest
a boy stares from the gas station office,
pop bottle hanging from his fingertip,
to consider the bluff across the river.
A poor view, but it's afternoon, and I submit
he sees all there is, certainly more than the tourist
from Maine or Missouri cajoling his camper
through heat to a change of scene.

If braying cicadas don't intoxicate,
if the box turtle killed by a low undercarriage
doesn't revolt, though the carapace is carved
from the flesh, you can afford to remember
that childhood moment when you, bored
watching summer inter your familiar world,
burned in a chair less comfortable
than available. Today you have in mind
something your atlas calls destination.
Leaving town, you press your hand
into the slipstream and force maturity's
demands down rack and pinion to the road.

The well-kept fences are kept up by the state
for your benefit. So you can forget your
misplaced dream of industrious farmers,
the thrift and neatness of local ethnic stock.
You can't get away with that sloppy thinking.
Long is a word pressed into service east
of mountains, the relief seen for sixty miles
only a mistake left to the hydraulic mercies

of some heavy equipment operator on summer pay.
Windrows supplant mountains, fade into each other
the way generations of beef compose themselves
upon the feedlots in Turneresque placidity.

Wind carries the cattle into your mind.
The packinghouse sigh of Sioux City covers
six counties of earth dike. Though you recognize
the pastoral hell we have improvised, the eye,
pleased against your will, wanders,
seeking that passionate landmark plowed under
a horizon which has long since encircled you
and waits only for night before closing in.

Walking to Work

Hungry for new road, today's rain
builds faster air for houses.
This recipe for a walk takes me
to the best stand of basswoods,
leaflets poking out from the furthest
leaves like cards shuffled and held
in the suspicious face of a house.
The owner seldom names his shade.
The hollow this house faces south
is the old truth of place mocked
in a new coat of paint, breathable
air from this slight ridge
spelling new contour to my stride.
Hunting dogs complain to game
forced urban in a whiff of prairie grass.

Petal-bruised lawns open news reports
I'd never have suspected: gentle
taxonomy of abuse—the child
pornographer parking his dull sedan,
opening the garage door by hand.
I know none of these people, only
their trees, perhaps a bass boat
trailered beneath them. An old schoolmate
could live behind these poplars,
wake from a Dutch dream to laureate
clouds fanning Ascension from his bedroom.
Sunlight deals a new hand and windows
reflect sky in a guarded visage
giving miles of nothing away.

Autumn Walk, the Old Neighborhood

Exponents add themselves to fuchsia
leaves delicate as prints Japanese masters
made temporary. Both outlasted
design and cruelty—aphorisms for this
fish market luck and diner decor. Dogs offer
bent flurries of yowl to screened porches.
Before winter I am paper impressed with leaves'
awkward chorus and tuned vapor. Paint
your houses, your sincere parrots,
but before waking the fences our fathers
destroyed with saplings, bend this wind
deeper into broken seats of parked cars.

When every deer has left the acreage
of our order, we must be smaller than
our trees, machines pumping referents
out their fibrous pores. That's it! Hard
as ice, the soon friend of buds fall feigns
toward us in cherry and nameless trees
reclined against a cardinal sky. No matter
our names are stolen from lost moths
flying into the windows after heat
wiggles off into space; we have it to give
and give we must if wonder relates to good
dirt of neighborhood play in name and fact.
This street could end at the canal. Why these
citizens question me I can't guess.

The Home I've Never Seen

is somewhere cold enough to turn the sea—
and it must be near the sea—that gray
of layered shale. The path to water, broken
as the one those Fuegan kids who rode
the Beagle with Darwin must have walked back
to their family's beatings and theft. I mean
Jemmy Buttons and his sister, Fuegan Basket,
so proud of their clothing. Nothing like
a garden, their home.
            Years later they adapted.
In Tierra del Fuego, European sailors lit fires
to stave off exposure. Sweating natives ran
hundreds of yards into the bite of wind
they bore without raiment. They'd banked
the sluggish fires within themselves so low
their only act was clamming. No mastodons for them:
no coats, no heat—no heat, no stories. Like
their ancestors, they waited at the shore.
This one, no ice would bridge. Each year the shells
piled deeper.
           I would have a fire, the breath
of glaciers hundreds of miles distant.
La Push would do, the local tribe resident
so long their name is sea—the cove's, the river's.
Each rock, a totem and a name. Mine would live
in dark fir's understory. I would call down
flocks with two low notes. A good chief would share
my name with stripes across his eyes, singing
from the last tree upright after storm:
Rain Never Blows Under His Coat.

In my ancient shack, a small stone grate,
a reasonable fire, the sound of fresh
water and only the greatest breakers.
Pole and beam, cedar shake, or a silver

trailer on concrete blocks so when I died
it could be rolled away. Unlike Li Po's
hermitage, no contention, no red guards
burn my front door to kill the poems
carved in it. If there weren't rot
enough in arboreal winds, I wouldn't build
of wood. Mold and fungus are citizens
too simple to corrupt. Rely on them.

Waves, of course, and waves of endless water
erase my poems from the beach. Why, reader,
do you think we call them drafts, and dread
giving them over? Again and again, our words
rewrite the wild calligraphy of claw
and hoof track alive in the hope you'll remember
or forget their meaning. You never do.

The schools persist to make one artist, maybe
one song or painting. How long do people creep
about on the edge of ice, at the edge of human
metabolism to wait for mastodons and stories?
How long live like poor Jemmy Buttons—
named for the purchase price his parents
could not use to fasten clothing, couldn't
even string. They made no string or tools
other than such sticks as Darwin later
saw birds use to pry ants out of holes.

Fuegans pried clams, took the Spanish name
for fire explorers saw by fooling themselves.

Fuegans used no fire, and lived despised
by their neighbors, successful Andes Indios,
textile savvy nomads and residents
of city-states, who could not even use
as slaves this hapless tribe, eternities
from Altamira. They painted nothing to
make a child entreat her father. *Papa, alta
mira! Toros Pintados!* What would they have
painted? Clams? How many red hearts drawn
on the cave wall, on photographs of deer
in the library book I check out?

How many times the target? How many gypsies
burn before Django Reinhart looks up
into the doctor's face to smirk: "So, you've
finally come, have you?" And we who've come late,
what will we leave ? a few videotapes? gnawed
bone? a sketch or equation to say we ate up all
the deer or light in our neighborhood
and still weren't satisfied, but "They were de-
licious/ so sweet/ and so cold."

Full Immersion Baptism

(Southern Missouri, Mid-August)

Big men wade into the jade reflections
of trees. This benison and oak-hickory forest
spells afternoon in a dry county. The white
shirt of the preacher (you assume) relents,
floats loose at his waist. Women have pinned
their full-skirted dresses between legs thick
and shapely as lathed wood. Cotton and flesh
slacken to water. What will later bind
now unclasps, as do the hands of faithful
ashore, unsure how close they want
or Christian love expects them to be.

What you can see of this from your car
poised on the one lane bridge planks—white
oyster of thigh and pinched red face fading
two feet down in water blue as black ink—
makes no sense. Rather, you make green
and highway stand for sense. You're on tour
for fish and atmosphere, for shortleaf pine,
release, and blood enough to take the tense
drive home. A strained discussion waits
for those who witness faith like this but can't
participate. This late, you may as well stay.

Above the river, road signs fade in sun
still hours from setting. Even grass is washed
in light or rain so harsh its color just
evaporates. You want to reach the interstate,
try for Kansas City or Memphis. Roll down
the window and let the warm breeze dry the sweat
from back of neck and hand. The shadows you escape
only now are rising from the blue holes.
Something in the singing warns you off.

This is not your home. No one knows you
here or wants to. Eighty's not too fast
to leave, saving them and yourself the sight
of faces through the water's blue pane,
the knowledge in them as they rise to greet you.

Remembered Shoreline

White stone of the lighthouse and white
wooden chapel ride green saddles
of hill or wave over the bay's
nervous chop. Birds, white and gray—
gulls, rock doves, the harrying terns—
call in the season of killing as
sun-bleached as shining slopes of hay
in the dry valleys a few miles
inland where the sea mist isn't
replanting the hillsides with grass,
air with loud, unnecessary
cries. Sheep grazing the coast hillsides
come near an edge held only by
the roots of grass and gorse above
the cliffs and the black basalt. Ache
of bright air to throb and echo
the darkest swell, and cormorants
drop, riding air displaced from waves'
leading edges—living the borders
with delicate foam they shadow
and mirror. One such silhouette dives
under the storm-green sky of a crest
thick with a flock of grunion. Standing
on the greased and rolling bearings
of cobble, a girl watches the take:
long bird neck snaking backlit
wave, caught forever in her memory,
fish crosswise in its bill. Suddenly
I enter this fable, standing
behind, all of us stuck in the pitch
of the mountainside pines—amber
for future observers to mine.

Maybe there is only one day
stitched together in the webwork

and lace of nerve and sea foam lattice,
making a redtail lift and light,
land and rise from the locust tree
outside my window as I try
to recall the sea, another
October Sunday decades later,
landlocked on a high plains river.
No, the hawk turns. Light takes its breast
and shadows enfold it in waiting.
Even here, sun's shallow attack
highlights feathered wood of window
casements bleached silver by summer
storms and heat. Here too, boys career
any offered slope on cardboard,
wood, dried cowhide, or stitch and rivet
pant seats. If no sheep restate clouds,
there are old men at their cards, so creased
into their squints they could be wind-
burnt Basques five hundred miles away,
playing mus beyond all sight of seas
since the Biscay freighter left them.

When I look up, the redtail's back,
the slope below her ripe with yearling
hares, plump does more afraid of winter
than her stoop. A silver kite hangs
from her elm. The leaves are barely
yellow. When we lived in the Coast
Range, I bathed early in fresh snowmelt.
A sudden weight added itself
to the buck just pulled from the hutch
as it slumped in death. Uncle Larry
twisted its neck. I used the club
to kill. A russet flash and the hawk
disappears between crowns of yellow
foliage. This locust light hurts
my bones. It always, always has.

Crossing the Equator at 40 Thousand Feet

As if we waited to be born
through steel and plastic skin,
two hundred of us loll under the portholes
in circles of moonlight
strained through thin cloud
too high for reflection in the sea below.
The lights of ships and stars
mingle indeterminate in a round world
ready to congeal. There is no earth
or other surface.

At my age and altitude
the stomach wants either calm
or turn. Show me the line, imagined
if need be, where pilot or navigator
warns us we are on our heads,
where we turn away from the old life
as my friend back home turns toward his
fortieth birthday—I see the number 40 in green
mile markers along some stretch of interstate.

The boundary where water, this free
juice, and booze begin to spin
counterclockwise through my guts
shifts each time. Knowing this
old-time sailors made of button
and string a model of the world to pass
the time: a whirligig that hummed
a shaky tune if one found the rhythm
of tension and release. On the first
crossing they shaved their heads,
came home with curls reversed,

    their parts migrating across their heads
    like the eyes of flounder.

We will return to divorce,
to thinning hair and the dictates
of fashion. We will sleep our way
into the new life without boundaries.
The sea is so vast we could lose
Australia, and even if we wished
we could not bring this flight down.

Dream of Black Water

The mouths of caves are not as dark,
nor is the water at their depths,
the glow of the lamps eking out
into the charisma of exact drops
sounding from all sides, in perfect,
separate time each the same fifty-four degrees..
In underground rivers, clear
to the antiseptic bottom, blind lizards
freeze in my beam, a moment
they cannot fathom. This water is black
and reflects black. What light
falls falls like water on waves
smooth and hard as metal.
I recognize no stars or reflection.

Darker too than MacRourie Harbor's
tannic waves. Tasmanian stars
stretched water for the South Pole.
A mountain range rode the morning sky
and shone from that surface.
Rocks rose up where guards chained
convicts at waterline in winter.

In the dream, I look up to land
flat as a grainy photo. I've traveled
weeks in a crooked salesman's
'52 Chevrolet. The people we cheated
have caught us and the car feels
gray against my back as if I'm pinned
in this camera. This paper develops

my head wrong. The bullet hole is wet
with fixative, my mouth open

to shock snapping my head
back from the lower jaw, eyes still
fixed on the man behind the rifle. I can't
feel my hands move in front of me,
trying to tell the laughing crowd
how to get out. Only I remember
the right road to the town where we
all lived before the black
water, the money.

Suitcases are red cattle on hills
come back to life in sun
out now by the lake where only I
dream, awake but crumpled before this car
the bride and groom drove from the wedding.
Still lost and numb, head shot, I stare
into my dream of that water.

Blowhole and Green Glass at the Apostles
— for Ken and Pat Anderson

If memory is sorry—storm flaying
miles of gorse, lighthouse
closed and roads so flooded
we walked on water—then tomorrow
must seem hopeful. Rainbows surfed
breakers onto rocks and I recall
the two of you blown up into the air
laughing after snapshots,
together after a family and a half.
Though the woman who introduced us
left me, nothing catastrophic there,
more the wearing away that cuts
spires off from the cliffs, slow.
Coves form waves to drill tunnels
back to blowholes with the sea's
strange rhythm in them. Boom,
and you think you've got it figured,
but it lowers the boom on you before
the last flume settles on the rocks.

The next day was antipodally clear,
winter's boon to visitors. I walked
the small harbor alone. While we slept,
the storm strangled a fairy penguin
in seaweed, its laced breast
mottled as if some bloom seeped out,
head skewed like a licentious girl's.
I thought of its journey from Antarctica

to burrows in sand dunes near your home.
A fishing boat leapt at its anchor chain

in swells still tall inside the breakwater.
Red spires called The Apostles I named
Peter, all of them. Under the meadow
where the shipwrecked are buried, minus
a woman saved by the sailor who didn't
know her name, we walked a chasm of wind
bridged by more red rock. Waves tossed up
green bits of glass ground velvet in sand
to lie wet and worthless in our hands.

A Field Guide to the Birds

Wedge-Tailed Eagles
    —Great Dividing Range, Australia

Not her cry nor the shadow
slipping and catching through the thin
canopy of gum leaf, but the very bird
echoed off rocks mouthed from earth
before dates, phrased as whale shape
and igneous lunge with a man's stance.
Our voices were only granite throwing
back the word she was, great depth
sloped against the sky.

Then two of them, and there was not
the sick turn of other than wing,
other than rock. Because they were
eagles, they were their world,
composed as much of cliff and light
as of grub and fat crested pigeon
with its cape of violet shimmer.

I've flown far from eagles, a man
with my single pair of feet on earth.
I've mailed myself into the wind.
What I cough up—skin, feather—
is all I am, a brutal eye for waste
of air or mind, no thought of gain.
Eagles do not eat on the wing.

Dunnocks on Norman Graves
—Lincoln Castle, 1993

A schoolboy, here to see how King John's seal
ate through the Magna Carta, peers down stairs
curled inside the tower. "My knees have all
gone to jam," he says. These stones are theirs

who lie beneath them, blanketed with grass
fine as English rain. Above one mound,
birds common as the row of council flats
built in the moat contend for higher ground.

The old name's "Shuffle-wing," from their display,
a shrug to claim their turf. Kings evict.
Domesday mentions families sent away;
counts an unnamed hundred sixty six.

No wind can starve this rain that still dissolves
men and limestone stacked in castle walls.

Guillemots on Cliffs

— Holyhead Mountain, Anglesey

Black and white, they look like puffins from
the RSPB tower's telescope.
Coins, a deck of two-toned cards thrown
against the wind, their luck prevents the stoop

of peregrines from ledges high above.
If one survives, ten die to add black
feathers and white flesh to the logic of waves
chopping tidal current beyond South Stack.

The summit's cairn of whitewashed stones supports
biting flies and half-imagined views
of Irish peaks. More stones imply the fort
cold Romans starved within. Returned, we muse

over our scones with whipped cream and jam,
how much like God there is about chance.

Corncrake in Flooded Fields At Hundred House
—June, 1993

Village paper reports townspeople kept
awake two nights by calls they couldn't name.
I come a week too late to hear its *Crex
crex*—"a wooden ruler on a comb,"

my field guide says. The only one in Wales,
perhaps, this summer of floods farmers wait
out in the pub, tense as these scarce rails
themselves, over scours and hay going to rot.

Jet fighters shave the hills as two dogs herd
cows unconcerned that farming change, change
of climate in the sub-Sahara pared
a dull bird's numbers in its summer range,

where people live and die between stone walls
and sleep in silence older than our laws.

Oystercatcher on Anglesea

Yellow tractors trailer small boats up
slate blue beach from bright and distant sea.
Channels water dug in sand now cup
three sloops. Skiffs are canted in the lee
of rocks or cradled just above high tide.
One speckled egg rests above a tidepool
red with bloom or blood.
                                   Intelligent stride
of a crow puts the oystercatcher's bill
in range of limpet and cockle. This bird may
live thirty years, will either pry or stab
its prey, and pass its genius on to young
it feeds, unlike other waders. Say
this old man stalks the beach, sagged
shoulders in a black coat, legs too long.

Raven in Matthew Price's Field, Hundred House

The English Robin leaves his thistle stalk
for gate, then hedge. Matthew says the land
means less each generation city folk
estrange themselves. Approach the just-lambed

ewes and six sheep dogs follow, old man
Price shouting them back out of high grass—
"Ye dairty boogers"—where goldfinches ride wind
out clasping a sheaf of seed-heads, red faces

aureoles around beaks. Though bull raises
a gale of grunt and bellow, and afterbirth
turns black in morning sun—fierce praise
rising like prayer and incense out of earth—

raven fans up above his prize, black
rag caught in wind's wheel, returns at a walk.

Kingbird

How often I wish to scream
like him, making the same point
in an old argument with hawk
or crow, taking on grackles
over the lawns of the rich
or strafing a pigeon for growing
fat in the graintowers
of some railroad town.

Today, a bored scholar,
I lean over the library table,
staring through sealed windows
across an archbishop's lawn.
Two dark angels dance off a pine
followed by a point I know
screams two-toned mojo on their backs,
perching to rip out feathers.

His name is Tyrant Flycatcher
and he works for it, blaming
himself for the world's
sleepy acquiescence. I watch
until he disappears, driving
crows like moneychangers
through the public park.

Winter Sonnet for an Absent Friend

Overhead, the sky clears and closes, clears
and opens lidlike on the earth, our gravid
map of missed appointments. At roadside, longspurs
deliberate with larks over a blush of spilled
corn and soy. Things are. We are not
satisfied with birds' currency, names
of days and months our calendars forget.
I want to force the truth out of you, scream,

but there is a field, a feedlot in front of me
and I'm alone with cattle scattered downhill
from the hayrick, their brown path in snow.
Because you are not with me, I test the icy
shoulder, scattering larks through a thrill
of fence and tree into air clearer than you know.

Paintings & Portraits

Homeplace

The house my grandfather built of local
pine and red oak, boards sawn
and cured in the back lot, his hand's
mark in plaster and tenon,
burned to its foundation.
The native sandstone
mortared in snaking lines of concrete,
veined grouting raised with the heel
of the trowel, stands as many
Ozark homes stand, far from help.
When I passed in red road dust,
a carload of kids swam
the stockpond, heedless of leeches'
taste for skin at flank
and back of knee. The fireplace,
a parapet without archer's notches
among new pines, Grandmother's
French doors, picture windows now,
cobbled into walls of salvage
board and tarpaper. A man measured
twice, sawed once if he were careful.
He nailed together a life.
Turkeys strut the road. Sumac clogs
the ditches, works through his forge
and rusting bellows. I have come
too late to be any help.

The Rapids
— After Winslow Homer

Seeing them in water color
puts together, piece by piece
the way I need to speak those simple
sentences of rock and liquid
light a river uses to tell
its best stories. Before the century
turned, a painter learned to escape
the isolation of friends to paint
what we are drawn to consider
horizon line across
rock and brush, a line that leads
to no resolution, that is
no help to the old friend
leaning toward me to whisper
as I draw away. Here is only
the smooth surface of the pool,
dark sheet of tension, blazed
with reflections of blue-white sky—
at once plainly brushstrokes,
and accurate—carried over
the spill unbroken. The precise
angle of logjams shows us how
composed we are, viewers on
our feet all day, soothed by arcs
of water, recurved spans of pure
space carved out of the pallet's
darkest shade, trail blazes
just axed onto wet bark.

On the banks alders do not
grow on south slopes of hollows
for the sake of composition,
to backlight conifer shadows
thrown by sober fir—
the angle of the under branches,
easy strokes for point of view.
I must trouble a good heart
with sandbars in half-light,
worry friends with talk of painters
who work temperature into the back
of camel hair brushes. Before
pressure jambs the blood, air
slips closer than a lover over my body.
I wear this good silk and step
guiltily out of the museum,
erased and redrawn into the long
shapes of current, obscure water
disappearing over the lip
of rock into light froth
shallows, into something to say.

A Font for Alison

> "...typography's glory is to serve
> the servants of the muse Erato..."
> — Harry Duncan

While we sleep together, our bodies
cast themselves into ligatures
till the sheets are impressed verso
and recto, and there's no telling
where your signature ends in mine.

When I wake before you, it is to study
you for a printer's patience.
You are composed in the separate
lights of a late winter morning.
Outside the window, sun cuts
ascenders of the Russian olive
into the stone wall, unjustified

and lovely as water. I want no bevel,
no face no shoulder or body or foot
but yours, only shadow serifs
below your lip, at underarm and rib.
Let me mouth this alphabet, palm it, give
you mine so that you may write
yourself across me. Your tablet,

I have gone all clayey, hands and feet,
must use the clumsy script and syntax
of my childhood to say how something
fierce I love you, must pull proof after
proof from my lips on your hair and eyelids
till I wake you to this musey service.

The Value of Art

This morning, having neglected
my obligations, I sit over my work
distracted by a small reproduction
of Renoir's Boating Party.
The canopy shading the subjects,
the painter's friends, blows in wind
arriving from the left and behind
the viewer, according to riffles
in the red and yellow canvas.
Light caught in table crystal
shunts through glass so that black
brushstrokes glaze the white surface.

What a menagerie of dress. How the ladies
hat themselves for summer. Sparrows
could build serviceable nests in these.
And if we care for hands, hands there are
in all attitudes. A man's and woman's
bivouac on a steep-backed chair,
a platoon of fingers. The straw-hatted
man reclines in a field of color,
his hand circumnavigating a dark waist.

"Spring," the young mona whispers
into the face of her terrier. And spring
worries his small black eyes,
varnishes the perfect arms of the man
seated behind her, a stevedore
who carried the canvas to the gallery.
This is all the France I need,
the palette of Renoir and my penance
of work waiting like a bright boat
beached as long as the party
sparkles in the foreground.

Mary Cassatt: The Bath

Water exists and is pure, but flesh
bathes in classical light,
porcelain basin and pitcher
splashed with reflection
off the body of the child, source
unfolded roughly into towel
and the dark, amorphous mother shape
within the periphery of her dress.

Flowers on the pitcher, toll painted
dresser and wallpaper roses
sprout from the red ground
of the carpet. Clay, fabric
and flower curve from water
to the composition of skin,
the clay-wet daughter leeching
light into that seasoned hand
her waist pinches off at wrist.
All flesh touches flesh:
mother's face to the shoulder
of the child whose hands balance
and bridge, one on a draped knee
next to the girdling hand,
the other at her own leg, linking
across the lacuna of white towel,
torso and the leg descending
to the operative palm that scrubs
her foot, the final circuit
engaging this feminine light.

And Cassatt... insulated at the end
of her brush from this coiled
spring of life, starting blind
at the woman's feet and ending
with two heads clustered above,
from the child's loose bangs, hair-tie
fixed in a shock of sable,
to the womanly sheen of steel blue
bun tightly centering the shadowed
turn of lidded eyes down to one
more shell of movement, the dawdle
of toes and the circling thumb....

Had she given in, painted with her
hair, fingernail for palette knife,
stretched wrist and eyelid skin
as canvas, she could not have born
more truly into light the continued
weight of children. Lines which are
no lines curve past the hands,
beyond the strands of mother hair
minutely loose. In all this repose,
no stopping but at one short
length of baseboard, a shadow
cupped in a single ear.

For the New Parents

When she cries you take her up
        like some remembered cause
or like a penny saved for luck,
        a shining statute laws
of chance can never quite revoke.
        And what can life this simple
require of you but that you hope
        your small gifts will be ample:
breath, a single body's warmth?
        You must release her now
to sleep and to the thousand harms
        of life and letting go.

Late Portrait of Robert

He would have been my father-in-law
for a few years, and then not,
had he survived his war dreams
of the alien Pacific. He lived
through stories, the suicide in photos
kept by my then-wife. How our
names for one another keep changing.

The electric shaver he'd used
his last morning came to me
like a nervous relic, wrapped in its
case and cord. The safety head
detached to spill a dusting of black
shavings across the sink. Even a man
as careful as he has lapses.

I imagine how, any other morning,
he would have cleaned the shaver
like any other machine, say, his
revolver, the small parts spread
on his palm as he plied the special
brush supplied with the case.
Instead, the shadow I had seen

under his cheekbone now lay
spread across the porcelain.
I knew I could not scrape his face
or mine free of stain, fine-grained
as the best gunpowder. Before I walked

out to face my wife and daughter
I looked in the mirror and shook out

another small charge into my palm.
If I could have held it tightly enough,
my fist might have become the casing
of a cartridge or a bomb. With the loaded
gun I had used so often as a boy
I raised my finger to my mouth,
aimed up into the darkness and fired.

The New Docent's Tour of Bathtub Madonnas, South Omaha

Bevels and columns define Italianate
leanings—no canals here, of course,
but visit the stockyards, and you'll find
gondolas: flatbed trailers and rail cars
high with cowhides folded in mitered piles.
We speak now of style, in any case, not the ethnic
culture—as easily Hungarian or Lithuanian…
But where was I?
                     Oh yes, leanings
toward sanitary worship, alabaster flesh. Note
the blue tattoo: "Standard Mfg. Chicago."
What was pursey is made round. The grotto
is stained rust where the meat packer lay
his blood matted head.
                        Concrete donkeys
resurrect themselves to render this boldly
stylized form. They wait out summer and fall
for the fiberglass virgin's touch. Not only bevel,
but quoin becomes less structural support
than medium when hundred watt bulbs turn nativity
to limpid essence of light. As if the Holy Family
ascended in radiant triumph from the snow,
all night is banished—
                               just as the cut and kill man
conquers debt and gravity to climb from flamingo-pink
bathwater, everyman rising above (dare we say it?)
the earthly bloodbath to clear a rough portal
in the steamed window glass with the ragged,
tumescent callus on the heel of his hand,
and declare for all the suddenly sober
house to know, his labor good.

Paris, a Rainy Day, Rue de This, Rue de That*

A reproduction from Chicago, where I saw
the original, French name, though if I tried
pronouncing it on the streets of the real
Paris, I'd get my face slapped. These aren't
even the turn-of-the-century streets
they pretend, but are wet in a dusty way.
The paving stones reflect diffuse
legs of a Parisian walking a woman
and umbrella toward another pedestrian.

The scene is poised at an awkward
encounter brought on by weather, by the man's
curled lip and the rustle of the crepe skirt
held in the woman's gloved hand. The tailor
left extra fullness in his left pant leg,
and his greatcoat falls with the weight
of quality to just above his knee. I don't
like that lip. If I were there, I'd pull
his mustache and plant a rude kiss
on his companion's thin mouth.

Some days the scene exists, some not.
Today, not. It is rainy. Paris, Chicago,
Omaha, Portland. She probably smells bad
in her black jacket of the what-*is*-that
style and her long skirts, hair

---

* After Gustave Caillebotte *Paris, A Dainy Day* (*Intersection of the Rue De Turin & Rue De Moscou*), 1877.

full of pomade, but a bad apple for all that.
None of the men carry anything in their
pockets, another reason they are not
real but only painted Parisians.

A Why-Not of Stones

It is a commonplace that river stones
tell stories, but I would like to know
more of this green one, veined,
with smooth hollows and twisted grooves,
ends shaped like hinges and bearings.

Why, when I am absorbed in their history,
am I so acceptable to the downy woodpecker
that he must startle me from the fir bough?
Though I have not learned the silence of stones,
I see the tanager's approach, and, no surprise,

chickadees hang nearby like ornaments.
Above me, the redstart orients herself
not with river or branch, but with the points
of the compass, turns like the rock
squirming in the little pocket it has found,
following others downstream.

When I see fieldstone, its colony of lichen
marking a hundred years of peace,
I think of the coast tribes' guardians.
An afternoon with Venuses at a local gallery,
and I am excused my stoniness, my slow,
awkward turning. Under the fields

they work toward sky by virtue of their own
integrity in the grip of ice.

A Heart Attack in the Men's Shower

I think, in my nakedness. Firemen, black boots
and coats shunting off the light, stand by law
at the scene. The formal composition
congealed in the shadowless frame of the showers
should be a painting by David. Nude men
lounge against tile, their legs abridged at knee
by uniformed attendants, the firemen's coats.

Centered in a shell of onlookers,
the victim coalesces like clouds of vapor.
He is pale as ceramic. Rented towels
drape him mid torso. Orange respirator cases,
electric paddles wait beside the stretcher.
Half out of picture, dark rows of lockers
where the eye rests upon yet more nudes,
their attitudes sketched in dim light. No one asks
the obvious question. In answer, a woman's voice
leaks from the firmament beyond the ceiling.

He's leaving..., she cries. Not one eye looks up
toward P.A. speakers where the only woman
tells us of her man. Any one of us may one day
find himself on that midnight train to Georgia,
or wherever we imagine home. If we don't believe
Gladys Knight, the Pips confirm our reservation.
We are indeed *leavinonat midnight train*. Not until
we all accept this difficult itinerary does
the man sit up, a colleague, too long in the newly-
repaired steam room—fainted in the shower.
He's older than me, paler and sweatier,
his cottage cheese complexion much like mine
in the dentist's chair the third time

my wisdom tooth broke, telegraphed
its pebbles-in-a-bag noise up my jaw.

The EMT eases him back against shower pipes,
mops sweat beads off his forehead, holds back
standing ranks of Davids and Adonises, the tank-
topped Hercules and towel-wrapped Wimpy. No one laughs.
The respirator snakes a tube across his upper lip.
The Whackem Pack is put away. When he stands again
among us, his blanched hand tracing the wall back
into the dark rows of our waiting clothes,
he's given us a day worth all the rest to seize.
None of us are big men in the world. However many
tiles we cover when we fall will have to
be enough, will all be about the same.

Execution
  — after Goya's 3rd *of May, Principe Prio*

Light plows furrows
in a Spanish night
where sheaves of peasants lie
stacked before French soldiers,
the harvest of diplomacy, of deals
made perhaps in the castle
standing dark now in the background.

A single star harrows a sky
blank as the soldiers' unseen faces.
They are merely ranks of shadow,
rigid teeth, rotten and biting
into the light-washed shirt
of the figure who flies

out of the brown and gold night
and into our memory, mouthing
the exact word neither we
nor Napoleon's men can translate.
His arms thrown wide,
he greets us all

from galleries of fine art and murder.
He paints for us a portrait
of our own fathers
grown coarse on hard labor,
broken without shame before us.

Art Homer has taught at the University of Nebraska at Omaha Writer's Workshop since 1982. He is the recipient of a 1998 NEA Writing Fellowship, a 1995 Individual Artist Fellowship from Nebraska Arts Council, and a Regents Professorship from the University of Nebraska. Homer's nonfiction book *The Drownt Boy: An Ozark Tale* (University of Missouri Press, 1994) was published as a finalist for the AWP Award in Creative Nonfiction. His previous three poetry collections include *Skies of Such Valuable Glass* (Owl Creek Press, 1990).

Printed in the United States
40493LVS00018B/172-207